MYSTERIES OF THE
ANCIENT
AMERICAS

BY SCOTT GILLAM

PEARSON
Scott
Foresman

Editorial Offices: Glenview, Illinois • Parsippany, New Jersey • New York, New York

Sales Offices: Needham, Massachusetts • Duluth, Georgia • Glenview, Illinois
Coppell, Texas • Sacramento, California • Mesa, Arizona

Who were the early Americans?

It is natural for us to be curious about the people who once lived where we now make our homes. Where did they come from? How did they live? What finally happened to them? To answer these questions scientists have been studying for decades what remains of the people who were the first to live in the Americas.

Beginning around 1930 many scientists believed that the original inhabitants of North America and South America first came to these lands about twenty thousand years ago over a land bridge between Siberia and Alaska. Scientists knew that early humans existed in Siberia during this period. The Bering Land Bridge, named after the body of water that now separates Siberia and Alaska, had been formed during the last Ice Age. When large amounts of ice formed, the sea level dropped, creating dry land between Asia and North America. These early humans were probably pursuing wild animals for food, clothing, and shelter.

The Clovis Connection

The single biggest source of evidence for the populating of the Americas was uniquely crafted spear points first found near Clovis, New Mexico, in the 1930s. Since then, similar points have been found in many parts of North America. Scientists dated the Clovis spear points as coming from a period beginning about 13,500 years ago. This was during the period in which early humans were entering the Americas over the Bering Land Bridge. Scientists concluded that the makers of these Clovis spear points had been the northern Asians from Siberia and their descendants, and that they were the first humans to enter North America and South America.

The Clovis people were hunters who thrived as long as there were large animals to hunt. As the large animals died out, early humans began to settle down, take up farming, and live in communities. Gradually, they learned to adapt to changing climates, which affected the water supply and the growing season. They were able to grow enough food to set aside some for future shortages. Surpluses meant that a group could now begin to trade with others for the things that they needed. Paintings and drawings like those found on pottery used to store food meant that some people now had more leisure time.

Leather straps were used to attach Clovis spear points to wooden sticks.

The Olmec: Earliest Empire in Mesoamerica

One of these descendants was the Olmec people. They began more than 3,000 years ago as farmers along the Gulf Coast of Mexico, just west of the Yucatan **Peninsula**. The Olmec created **aqueducts** to transport drinking water. As a settled farming group, the Olmec advanced enough as a culture to support artists who created giant sculptures. These huge stone works were probably transported by water from their place of origin to the Olmec capital at La Venta, more than fifty miles away. The Olmec also designed buildings that represented Olmec religious beliefs. We do not know how the Olmec finally met their end. Was it due to an enemy or to disease? Whatever the cause, it seems clear that the Olmec greatly influenced their Maya descendants.

Olmec figurines, such as this one of a baby, may have been offerings to the Olmec gods.

Mayan Civilization

Historians disagree on exactly when Mayan civilization began and where it came from. Some historians think that Mayan culture may have begun over 4,000 years ago. This would mean that the Maya and the Olmec lived side-by-side for a time. Other historians think that Mayan society began around 1,000 B.C. It is possible, but not certain, that the Maya developed out of the Olmec civilization. What is known for certain is that Mayan civilization led to many cultural, scientific, and political achievements. The Mayan calendar, astronomical records, and method of writing on bark paper, or **codex**, were highly advanced. The Maya occupied territory in what are now Mexico, Guatemala, Belize, Honduras, and El Salvador.

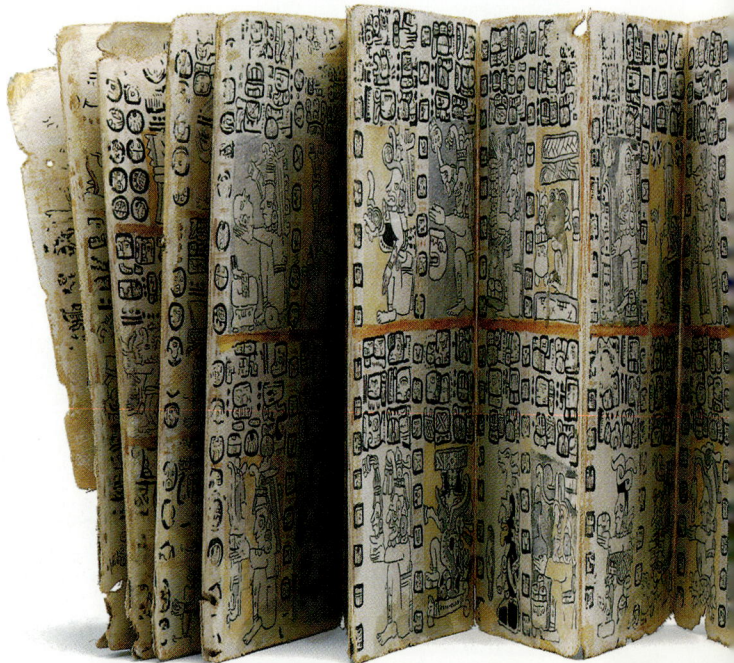

Why did the Maya disappear?

As with many historical questions, there is no single answer as to why the great Maya civilization fell. There is, instead, a combination of factors. There was tension between neighboring cities in the Maya Empire and between the wealthy and the poor. Expanding populations also overused the rain forest and were very dependent on a weak water supply. Famine and disease would have also taken a toll, as would any outside invasion. Together, two or more of these factors likely led to the end of the Maya Empire.

Mayan bark-paper books contained information for Mayan priests, such as material on predicting the future. Characters were written or painted with brushes on long strips of bark paper that was folded into an accordion-like book, and covered in a layer of chalky paste.

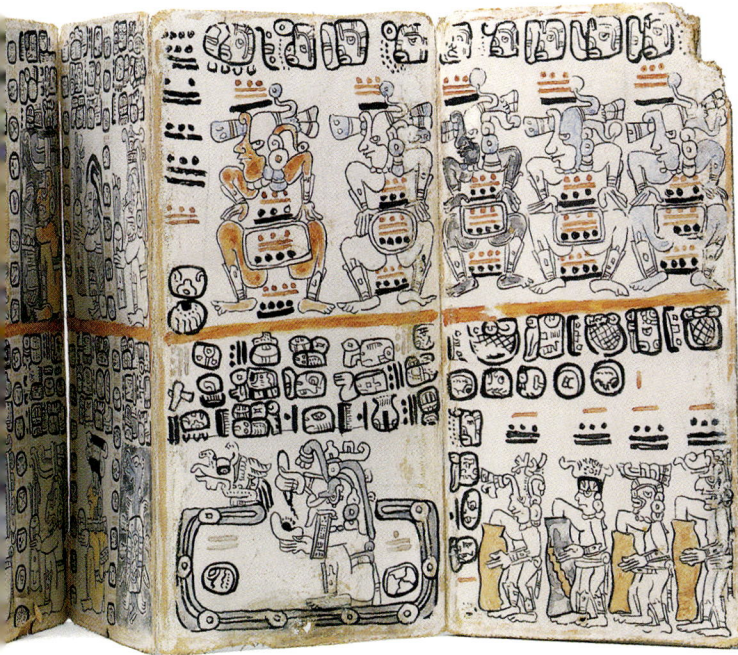

The Rise and Fall of the Aztec

Like the Olmec and Maya who came before them, the Aztec were basically a farming culture. Their ancestors were said to have migrated from a place in northwestern Mexico known as Aztlán (ahz-TLAHN) around A.D. 1000. According to Aztec myth, the war and sun god Huitzilopochtli (WEE-tsee-lo-poacht-lee) urged the Aztec to migrate. The Aztec capital, Tenochtitlán (te-noch-tee-TLAHN), in the Valley of Mexico was established in A.D. 1325. Tenochtitlán was an island to which the Aztecs added **chinampas**, all connected by **causeways**. By forming a loose **alliance** with some peoples and conquering others, the Aztec created a vast empire that may have numbered five million.

The Spanish defeated the Aztecs in 1521. The Aztec's weak political structure and weapons were no match for the Spaniards' military tactics, steel swords, muskets, cannons, and riders on horseback. Disease also greatly reduced the Indian population. Today we learn about Aztec culture mainly from archaeological finds. Some Aztec descendants still prepare food in traditional ways. Mexican Spanish contains Aztec words, such as *tomato*, *chile*, and *tamale*, that have also become part of the English language. Mexican artisans still make traditional pottery and textiles that hint of the lost empire.

Religion was central to the Aztec way of life. Aztecs believed that their world would end unless human sacrifices were made to the sun god.

Pre-Incan Civilizations: The Moche

The earliest empire in the Americas, the Moche, developed around A.D. 100. The Moche (MOH-cheh) united the city-states along the coast of Peru to form the Moche Empire, which was about the size of the state of Vermont. Despite its desert environment, the Moche Empire supported a population of about 100,000 at its peak. The Moche people survived by fishing the coastal waters and by irrigating their fields with water from the many rivers that drained into the Pacific Ocean. Over several hundred years the Moche evolved into a highly artistic culture despite a harsh political system.

Possible Environmental Disaster Victims?

The Moche may have come from Central America. Their end probably began when a lengthy drought (and possibly an earthquake) hit the area, followed by flooding caused by El Niño. El Niño is a weather pattern that regularly brings warm water to Peru's coast. Flooding probably washed away much of the topsoil on which Moche farms depended. At the same time, strong offshore winds would have blown sand from the coastal beaches over the fields. These events made it even more difficult to grow crops and forced the Moche to move north along the coast. El Niño events also do great harm to any people who rely heavily on fishing coastal waters because the water becomes much warmer and fish die. These are some of the reasons why the Moche had disappeared by about A.D. 800.

Moche pots showed the social level or occupation of a person, shown here by the type of clothing and the decorations.

The Origin and Fate of the Inca Empire

Between A.D. 1100 and 1200 and seven hundred miles south of the Moche Empire site, the much more powerful Inca Empire was beginning. This empire eventually grew along the Pacific coast to include an area equal to the size of Western Europe. Although the Inca had no system of writing, extensive records and measurements were recorded on **quipus** (KEE-pooz). However, our knowledge of early Inca history remains unclear. The Inca Empire expanded from its first major city, Cusco, which is located in Peru, approximately 200 miles northwest of Lake Titicaca.

The end of the Inca Empire is somewhat better documented than its origins. In 1532 the Spaniard Francisco Pizarro (fran-SEES-koh pee-SAHR-roh) and his small army defeated the Inca, aided in large part by the smallpox that was already widespread on the continent, and killing millions of people who lacked immunity to the disease. Pizarro arrived during a bitter power struggle between two brothers in the Inca royal family. Seeing a way to further divide the already weakened Inca, Pizarro deceived and executed Atahualpa (ah-tah-WAL-pah) the brother who had been on the verge of victory in the civil war. Pizarro was then able to defeat the Inca without a major battle. Pizarro's main problem now was not conquest but maintaining his control of the conquered Incas.

Inca panpipes could be made of cane, clay, or quills from the feathers of a condor, a large bird of prey. The most common Inca instruments were percussion instruments, such as the drums, or wind instruments, such as the panpipes or flute.

The Anasazi: Ancient Ones of the Southwest

The Anasazi (ah-nuh-SAH-zee) people, who dug the **pit houses** and built **pueblos** of sandstone and **adobe**, began about A.D. 100. It is possible that the Anasazi may have developed from an older culture called the Mogollon (moh-GOH-yohn) that existed in east central Arizona and west central New Mexico beginning at least as early as 100 B.C. Originally the Anasazi were nomadic hunter-gatherers. After they learned to grow squash and corn, they began to build more substantial homes, such as the multi-story pueblos that still survive today.

Was it only drought that finally drove the Anasazi from their homes in the late 1200s? They had survived dry spells in the past. Why not this one? Some archaeologists think a dramatic cooling trend or sudden unpredictable weather kept the Anasazi from growing food at either high elevations that were too cold or low ones that were too dry. Others believe conflict over land and water rights may have led to wars. Still others see a religious crisis since the Anasazi did not re-create their old religious symbols in the new places they moved. There may be some truth to all these theories.

The original Anasazi left suddenly, but their descendants still live in the same area of the United States. These Pueblo in Acoma, for example, live in one of the oldest continuously inhabited communities in the United States. Pueblo have been living there since the 1100s.

Looking Back at the Question of Origin

We have seen how different some of the various groups of early American peoples were from each other. Scientists are always making new discoveries and discovering new techniques for finding out more about our earliest ancestors. In 1996 some 9,000-year-old remains—since named Kennewick Man—were found near the Columbia River in Washington State. Recent studies by scientists on Kennewick Man and his origins remain unclear. Other equally surprising discoveries probably lie ahead.

Glossary

adobe building material made of mud and straw that is dried in the sun

alliance an agreement made between two or more groups or nations

aqueduct a structure used to carry flowing water from a distance

causeway a raised bridge made of land

chinampa a man-made island

codex a folding-screen book containing information about predicting the future and religious rituals

peninsula land that is nearly surrounded by water

pit house a house made from digging a hole in the ground and covering it with logs

pueblo a structure of adobe brick

quipu a knotted rope used by the Inca to keep records